4

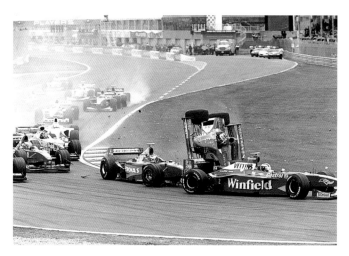

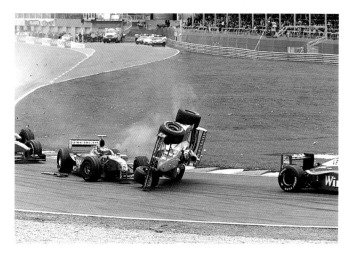

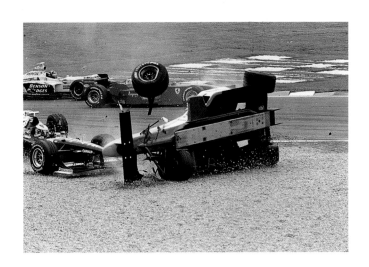

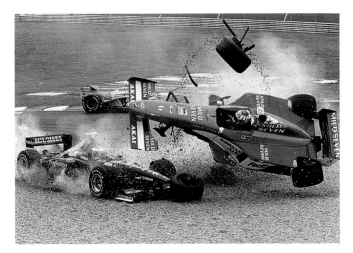

VISIONS OF

ALLSPORT

ALLSPORT • UNIVERSE

We would like to thank Graham Rutherford and Mark Reynolds of Fujifilm Professional for their continued support and assistance on the Visions of Allsport project.

Picture Researchers: Brandon Lopez, Neil Loft, Tony Graham, Darrell Ingham, and Jon Berisford

Writers: Chris Beeson and Kate Donovan

First published in the United States of America in 1998
by UNIVERSE PUBLISHING
A Division of Rizzoli International Publications, Inc.
300 Park Avenue South
New York, NY 10010

Copyright © 1998 Allsport Photographic

ISBN: 0-7893-0223-3
Library of Congress Catalog Card Number: 98-61199

Design by Mirko Ilić Corp.

Printed and bound in Singapore

8

Front Cover:
Skyward bound: Kristie Marshall of Australia at the 1997 Freestyle World Championships in Nagano, Japan, on February 6, 1997. (Mike Powell)

Back cover and flaps:
See pages 24, 40, 102, 111, and 141.

Page 1: Allez les bleus! Youri Djorkaeff of France lifts the trophy as France defeats Brazil 3-0 in the 1998 World Cup Final at Stade de France, St. Denis, France on July 12, 1998. (Shaun Botterill)

Page 2: England's David Batty and Tunisia's Imed Ben rise to the challenge in the 1998 World Cup Finals in Marseilles, France. England defeated Tunsia 2-0. (Stu Forster)

Page 3: Jero Shakpoke of Nigeria flies over Alfonso Perez of Spain in the 1998 World Cup Finals in Nantes, France. Nigeria defeated Spain 3-2. (Shaun Botterill)

Page 4-5: No stunt car here: Alexander Wurz's spectacular crash on the first lap of the 1998 Canadian Grand Prix in Montreal, Canada. (David Taylor)

Page 6, clockwise from top left:

Ronaldo shows who's boss as Inter Milan defeats Lyon 3-1 in a second leg, second round, UEFA Cup match in Lyon, France. (Frederic Nebinger)

South Africa's Brian McMillan is out to Australia's Mike Kasparowicz in the Australia versus South Africa first test in Melbourne on December 28, 1997. (Brian Radford)

Sore loser: Jamaica's second-place finisher looks away as Gail Devers basks in Olympic glory after her victory in the 100-meter final in Atlanta on July 27, 1996. (Gerard Vandystadt)

Flying high: Sergei Bubka successfully pole vaults to his fifth World Championship title, in 1995 at Goteborg, Sweden. (Gary M. Prior)

Page 7, clockwise from top left:

Giving him a run for his money: Benny the Dip, with Willie Ryan aboard (right), won the 218th English Derby on June 7, 1997, in a photo finish over Silver Patriarch, ridden by Pat Eddery (left). (Phil Cole)

¡Viva La España! Marathoner Alberto Juzdado is greeted by gold medal-winner Martin Fiz and Diego Garcia in second giving Spain a 1–2–3 finish at the 1994 European Championships at Helsinki, Finland. (Clive Brunskill)

British Boxer Lennox Lewis's acrobatic celebration of his second round TKO of American Oliver McCall for the WBC Heavyweight belt on September 30, 1994, at Wembley Arena. (John Gichigi)

Whooping it up: Kevin Brown and Charles Johnson of the Florida Marlins celebrate their 7–4 victory over the Atlanta Braves on October 5, 1997, at Turner Field in Atlanta, Georgia. (Jed Jacobsohn)

Page 8: The cold shoulder of defeat: George Perry of the USC Trojans at LA Memorial Coliseum in Los Angeles, California, on November 22, 1997. The Trojans lost to the UCLA Bruins 24–31. (John Ferrey)

Page 9: Hot wheels: Moretti racing at Le Circuit de la Sarthe in Le Mans, France, June 1997. (Mike Hewitt)

Los Angeles Lakers superstar guard Magic Johnson celebrates his victorious return to the NBA. Johnson, who retired from basketball on November 7, 1991, after testing positive for the HIV virus, totaled 19 points, 10 assists, and 8 rebounds in the Lakers' 128–118 victory over the Golden State Warriors on January 30, 1996. (Al Bello)

Jumping for joy: American Tom Lehman chips in a birdie at the 15th hole, but loses the match in an eventual European 14–13 victory at the 1997 Ryder Cup in Valderrama, Spain. (Jamie Squire)

• Golf is amongst the slower-moving games, and hard golf action appears less frequently than in most sports. When a winner is celebrating, it is a welcome contrast to the more standard shots of golfers framed against stunning landscapes.
• Caddying one's own camera equipment around a golf course for up to fourteen hours a day (often in grueling heat) takes true stamina on the part of a photographer.

The spitting image: A racer passes over a decorative chalk drawing of a cyclist in the 11th stage of the 1995 Tour DuPont. (Pascal Rondeau)

Bird's eye view: Pitcher Kevin Ritz of the Colorado Rockies gets ready to release the ball at home in Coors Field in a 7–3 loss to the San Diego Padres during the 1997 season. (Brian Bahr)

p. 14–15: Making the most of home turf: Yankees pitcher David Cone stretches before a game on top of the NY logo behind home plate at Yankee Stadium in the Bronx. (Al Bello)

p. 16–17: Sound sleeper: A young boy sleeps undisturbed as 29,000 runners go by in the 1997 London Marathon. (Craig Prentis)

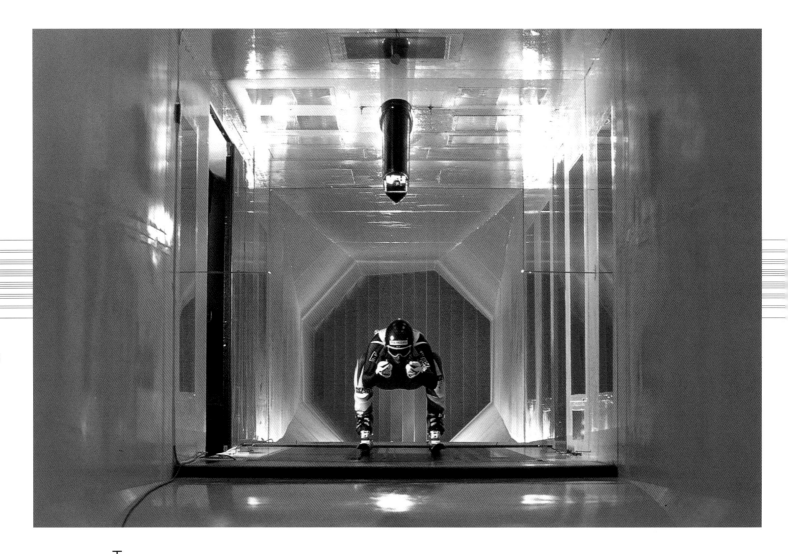

The British ski team's Graham Bell tests the Jordan F1 air tunnel in search of the best possible aerodynamic position for hurtling down a mountain. (Michael Cooper)

Out of context: Manchester United star David Beckham lined up for a soccer commercial. (Alex Livesey)

p. 20–21: The extravagant opening ceremony for the 1994 Winter Olympic Games in Lillehammer, Norway. (Gerard Vandystadt)

A moment of goodwill before the game: Bolivia defeated Mexico 3–1, before eventually losing in the finals to Brazil, in 1997's Copa America, South America's most important soccer championship. (Mark Thompson)

23

Joyride: Japanese driver Shinji Nakano of Team Prost Mugen-Honda finished only 11 laps of the 62-lap San Marino Formula One Grand Prix at the Enzo and Dino Ferrari circuit on April 27, 1997, in Imola, Italy. (Michael Cooper)

FOREWORD

To celebrate thirty years of the Allsport photographic agency, we have produced a book displaying the variety and quality of our work. Visions of Allsport features all that is best from the portfolios of the Allsport photographers over the last few years. It is a collection of exciting new work, much of which continues to push the acknowledged boundaries of sports photography and the way in which we view sporting events.

Many people may ask: Where is the classic photo of this or that event? These key moments of people and places all exist in the very extensive Allsport library, but we have deliberately chosen images for this book that represent the farthest parameters of sports photography rather than the most famous events.

As well as celebrating thirty years of Allsport, 1998 is also the year when Allsport became part of Getty Images Inc. Getty Images is the most comprehensive source of imagery in the world, and Allsport is proud to help contribute to the quality and creativity of this group. This

John Bentley of the British Lions flattens South Africa's Pieter Rossouw in an 18–15 Lions win on June 28, 1997. (Dave Rogers)

partnership has opened up the way to the next century, and we look forward to the continued success of Allsport thirty years from now. The future of sports photography is as tremendously exciting as the future of sports itself. No doubt technology will play an increasingly important part in the way that Allsport photographers create their pictures. New technology will also play an important part in the ways in which people will view Allsport pictures. In short, the future of great sports photography knows no bounds.

I would like to thank Fuji for its support in helping to bring this book about. Without them and the other leading brands in the photographic industry, ours would be a very difficult job indeed.

Steve Powell
Chairman and Chief Executive Officer, Allsport Photographic

Two wrestlers struggle parallel to the ground in a Greco-Roman Wrestling match on June 28, 1995. (Gerard Vandystadt)

Ernie Els plays from the reeds in the 1996 Johnnie Walker Super Tour in November. (David Cannon)

Yves Kruzio of Switzerland in his 11th place final run at the 1995 World Championship Men's Slalom Waterskiing on September 17 at Roquebrune-Argens, France. (Richard Martin)

Making a splash: Australian Daniel Kowalski swims to the fastest qualifying time at the 1994 World Swimming Championships in Rome. (Simon Bruty)

• Water is a medium that allows a photographer to achieve a variety of effects. Because it is fluid, translucent, and reflective, each frame of a swimmer will reveal a new and different feature. As seen here, the disturbance of the water often frames the action of the swimmer.

29

Boxing promoter Don King's hair stands on end (as it usually does) for the weigh-in before Mexican junior welterweight Julio Cesar Chavez lost a twelve-round decision to American Frankie Randall in January 1994. (Al Bello)

Total eclipse: A snowboarder leaps into the light before a crowd of spectators at the 1995 World Championships. (Michael Cooper)

American phenom Tiger Woods and his gallery watch him finish a disappointing 12 strokes off
the lead at the 1997 British Open at the Royal Troon Golf Club. (David Cannon)

Beads aflight: Seventeen-year-old American Venus Williams on her way to a 7–6 (7–5), 4-6, 7–6 (9–7) semifinal win over Romanian Irina Spirlea, before losing two days later to Martina Hingis in the 1997 U.S. Open finals. (Al Bello)

33

Athletics infielder Scott Spiezio stands out in a 7–3 victory over the Anaheim Angels in Anaheim near the end of the 1997 baseball season. (Harry How)

PERSONAL BEST

No sleight of hand here: These might be the white-gloved hands of a juggler or magician but they belong, in fact, to a World Snooker Championship referee at the Crucible Theater in 1992. (Howard Boylan)

p. 38-39: Straight to the jaw: English heavyweight Henry Akinwande on his way to a 27-0 record with a ten-round decision over American Tony Tucker on December 12, 1995, at the Spectrum in Philadelphia. (Simon Bruty)

Prince Naseem Hamed does a victorious handstand after stopping fellow Briton Billy Hardy in the first round to retain the IBF and WBO featherweight titles on May 3, 1997. (John Gichigi)

I AM PRINCE NASEEM HAMED

—undefeated, champion featherweight of the world. Some people think I'm outspoken, too much talk. They said the same about great champions like Ali, Hagler, and Leonard—it didn't bother them either. If I am outspoken it's because there's a lot I want to say—self-publicity has been an important part of our sport since the Louisville Lip captured the media. Too much talk? I believe I've got the action to justify my words and a 100 percent record to prove it. I've got the belts, and I'm determined to keep them.

Every time I've fought, I have been blessed with a win. Every time I win, I'm all over the world's sports pages, so I'm well used to seeing myself frozen in time. Often it's Allsport that captures these explosive Naz knockout moments. I've worked with many of the Allsport guys— John Gichigi has been shooting me since the early stages of my career, and Al Bello helped to

make my U.S. debut as spectacular as it was with some excellent publicity shots. But once I spring over the ropes into the kingdom of the ring, everything outside ceases to exist. I don't see the flash of photography or the TV cameras—the crowd fades to background noise. My entire world consists of myself and the man who's come to test me. In that moment of total focus, there's no way I can lose.

It's all about being the best in the business. I've seen myself, 60 feet tall, looking out over New York from a billboard. That's how I feel every time I fight, every time I live up to my own hype, and every time I raise my gloves, still undefeated. As my reputation grows, it gets harder to hide from me, harder to deny that I'm the best featherweight in the world. Take your pictures and spread the word.

Prince Naseem Hamed

ANYONE WHO SAW THE EPIC BATTLES

between Muhammad Ali and Joe Frazier or followed the exemplary career of Henry Cooper will have recognized that boxing can have a bizarre nobility. Man has voluntarily been fighting man for laurel crowns or lucrative purses since the days of ancient Greece. I instinctively bridle against those political correctors who would ban us from doing anything while it remains statutorily legal.

Obviously the foregoing will be dismissed as irresponsible by the medical profession, and there is no gainsaying their objections. Boxing may well have been the passport from the ghettoes for some young men otherwise destined for skid row or worse, but there is abundant evidence that it must also answer for premature deaths and catastrophic physical disability, none more so than in the case of Muhammad Ali himself.

Evander Holyfield's bloodied ear—or what was left of it—after Mike Tyson was disqualified for biting off the missing section during their heavyweight rematch at the MGM Grand Garden in Las Vegas, Nevada, on June 28, 1997. (Jed Jacobsohn)

As in motor racing, skiing, bullfighting, even rugby nowadays, professional boxing is a career in which a man must weigh risk against the possibility of vast reward and, for me, until even a few years ago, this was a perfectly viable option. Now I am not so sure, and one of the reasons is illustrated in the photo accompanying these words.

This is simultaneously one of the most brilliant, nauseating, and damning shots ever captured by a sports photographer. There are no prizes for guessing that in its sickening awfulness it depicts what was left of Evander Holyfield's right ear only seconds after Michael Tyson had sunk his teeth into it when facing defeat in their return world heavyweight title fight in Las Vegas.

Like me, thousands previously ambivalent about boxing felt enough was enough. We had never been sufficiently naïve to believe that boxing has anything to do with the noble art of self-defense—it hadn't been for at least two centuries, if ever—but here was stark visual evidence of its descent into decadence. Millions of dollars rested on the outcome of that fight.

It was the nadir of an accelerating decline from the moment a few businessmen—a euphemism for what I really mean—realized that the new El Dorado was to link up boxing with global television for enormous fees, to create four divisions at every weight and thus provide vicarious entertainment for home audiences every Saturday night. Only the truly stupid would fall for such hype when so many of these encounters have been blatantly fraudulent mismatches ending in seconds rather than rounds.

Ian Wooldridge, The Daily Mail (London)

Six months after his unforgettable bout with Tyson, heavyweight champion Evander Holyfield
poses for this photo taken in Atlanta in December 1997. (Al Bello)

43

A twenty-one-year-old Tiger Woods celebrates his 1997 Masters victory with a par putt for an 18-under-par 270 at the Augusta National Golf Club, the lowest score ever shot at the Masters. (David Cannon)

Nick Faldo contemplates his second shot to the 13th green at the 1996 Masters on his way to a closing 67 for a 12-under-par 276, taking the winner's green jacket away from Greg Norman. (David Cannon)

SPRINGTIME IN GEORGIA.

There is nowhere like Augusta and there is no tournament like the Masters. It was the vision of Jack Nicklaus strutting across this extraordinarily colorful stage that inspired me to take up golf. That was almost thirty years ago. I remember sitting transfixed in front of a television set at my parents' home in Hertfordshire. "What a way to make a living," I thought, "What a life!"

From that moment I pretty much dedicated myself to golf. Countless hours on the practice ground were followed by countless hours on the putting green. If I placed two balls on the green, one of the putts I lined up was always: "This one for the Open"; the other was to win the Masters.

The television images didn't lie. My first visit to Augusta came in 1979. Like any first timer, I was dazzled by the sheer beauty and brilliance of the place: Magnolia Drive, Amen Corner, the Par Three Course, the azaleas and dogwoods, and those wonderfully manicured—and unbelievably green—fairways.

The ambience is so charming, so graceful, and yet it has the capacity to completely numb your senses. It is as if when you speak you feel compelled to whisper. Everywhere you turn there are reminders of the great champions, the Augusta legends: of Bobby Jones who created the event; of Gene Sarazen and his "shot heard around the world"; of Ben Hogan, the finest ball striker the world has ever known; and of Jack Nicklaus, the winner of six Green Jackets. It is all quite magical.

If the setting is incomparable then the tournament itself has produced a disproportionate

level of drama. Indeed, the Masters seems to generate as many thrilling finishes as the other four major championships combined. The cause of this is, of course, Augusta's storied back nine, and holes through 11–13 (Amen Corner) in particular.

A potentially perilous downhill approach at the 11th, where you must avoid a pond that eats into the left half of the green (guess where the pin is placed on Sunday afternoons!) is followed by the par three 12th, surely the world's most terrifying short hole. Framed by tall pines, the wind swirls directly above an exceptionally shallow green, which is defended by both water and

sand. My caddie Fanny Sunnesson reckons it is the only hole where she prays on the tee. And then comes the stunningly beautiful 13th, perhaps the finest and most strategic par five in golf with its "do I, don't I" second. Rae's Creek runs in front and along the right-hand side of the green, where many Masters hopes have met a watery grave.

Augusta and Amen Corner have been very kind to me over the years. In 1990, I lived my boyhood fantasies when I partnered Jack Nicklaus in the final round en route to successfully defending my title. This photograph was taken just moments before I struck the best long-iron shot of my life—a 2-iron from a hanging lie at the 13th during the final round of the 1996 Masters.

N ick Faldo

True to form, Greg Norman tees off at the Player's Championship at Ponte Vedra Beach, Florida, on March 27, 1997. (Andy Redington)

Mary Pierce of France finishes a forehand at the 1997 French Open at Roland Garros, where she was knocked out in the fourth round by Monica Seles. (Mike Hewitt)

48

Second-seeded American Michael Chang serves on his way to a 6–2, 6–3, 6–2 first-round win over Rodolphe Gilbert of France at the 1997 French Open. (Stephane Kempinaire)

- With a professional tennis match lasting anywhere from just over an hour to more than five hours, a photographer can never predict how long he will have to get the best pictures.
- To catch the player in the serving action, the photographer must be ready a moment before the player releases the full impact of racquet on ball.

Australian Mark Philippoussis served up 29 aces to defeat then top-ranked Pete Sampras
6–4, 7–6 (11–9), 7–6 (7–3) at the 1996 Australian Open. (Clive Brunskill)

- When the ball is served, it can reach speeds up to 149 mph at its fastest, making impact shots with the ball in the frame that much harder to shoot.
- Tennis stadiums stand towering over the courts so that contrasts in sunlight and shadow create a challenging problem.
  To enhance the color of such powerful images as these shown here, a photographer will use a slow 50 ASA transparency film.

Not for the faint of heart: Bungee-jumping over Chelsea Bridge in London on May 30, 1997. (Craig Prentis)

When joy knows no bounds: German Udo Quellmalz celebrates in midair after defeating Japan's Yukimasa Nakamura for the gold medal in the men's half-lightweight judo competition at the Atlanta Olympics. (Simon Bruty)

p. 52–53: Far above the smooth blue surface, Troy Dumas of the USA takes flight in this spectacular dive to become the Junior Olympic champion. (Mike Powell)

Richard Krajicek drops to his knees in joyous disbelief after becoming the first Dutchman to ever win a Grand Slam event, defeating American Malivai Washington 6–3, 6–4, 6–3 at Wimbledon in 1996. (Gary M. Prior)

British boxer Prince Naseem Hamed celebrates after knocking out American Tom "Boom Boom"
Johnson at 2:27 of the eighth round to bring his record to 25–0 and unify the WBO
and IBF featherweight titles on December 8, 1997. (Mark Thompson)

"The world's strongest man," Russian Olympic gold medalist Andrey Chemerkin celebrates a successful lift in Atlanta in 1996. (Simon Bruty)

57

Head to toe: Chinese gymnast Xuan Liu displays her flexibility at the 1996 Atlanta Olympics. (Mike Powell)

Peter Novak of Czechoslovakia scores only a 7.925 on the rings on his way to a 76th-place finish at the 1994 World Gymnastic Championships in Brisbane, Australia. (Richard Martin)

Kazakhstan's Igor Potapovich pole-vaults against a dramatically flame-lit sky to a fourth-place finish in Atlanta's Olympic Stadium in 1996. (Mike Hewitt)

Fu Mingxia of China prepares to dive for her gold medal at the IX Diving World Cup on September 7, 1995, in Atlanta, Georgia. (Jamie Squire)

• In the Olympic high dive, the photographer must freeze the most dramatic moment as the diver drops ten meters at dizzying speed.
• The divers have three attempts to achieve the perfect dive, allowing the photographer three blink-of-the-eye opportunities to capture the perfect shot.

A giant "doughnut" of a diver somersaults through the air for the judges at the men's three-meter springboard competition at the Atlanta Olympics. (Stu Forster)

• The background in a diving shot is extremely important in keeping the diver from being lost in the frame. Stu Forster used a slow shutter-speed to create the blurred doughnut effect of this shot while focusing on the crowd behind.

Icy resolve: An intrepid climber takes on an ice-covered peak in the falling snow. (Ian Tomlinson)

A climber scales a Brazilian cliff against a spectacular background of gushing falls at the 1997 World Nature Games. (Simon Bruty)

Sweden's Michael Jonzon shows off his swing against a dramatic backdrop of snowcapped peaks at the 1995 Canon European Masters in Crans sur Sierre. (David Cannon)

A game of badminton, Indonesia's national sport, is played at Borobudur, regarded as the largest Buddhist temple in the world. (Simon Bruty)

With her gold-medal-winning performance of 5.8s and 5.9s in her free program at Nagano, American Tara Lipinski became the youngest individual Winter Games gold medalist ever. (Matthew Stockman)

The best seat in the house: IOC President Juan Antonio Samarach watches the Opening Ceremony of the 1998 Winter Olympic Games in Nagano, Japan. (Richard Martin)

69: The unbeatable moment of victory: Italy's foil team defeats Romania for the 1996 Olympic gold medal in Atlanta. (Stu Forster)

WINNING

Poised for speed: USA sprinter Michael Johnson's signature golden shoes at the 1996 Atlanta Olympics. Johnson became the first man ever to win gold in the 200 and 400-meter races, shattering a world record in the former. (Gary M. Prior)

• A race like the 100-meter sprint gives a photographer less than ten seconds to discern who the winner will be and to get a shot showing the energy and brilliance of a record-breaking performance.

TIMES

REFLECTIONS IN A GOLDEN EYE: SPORT AND THE MEDIA OVER THE PAST THIRTY YEARS

The rather grandiose title above begs a significant question: Through whose eye is modern sport predominantly seen, interpreted, and portrayed? Is it still the admiring eye of the live spectator? Surely not; those days passed long ago. Is it the discerning gaze of the astute reporter and the quicksilver sports photographer? Probably not; their halcyon days may also have passed. Today, sport is presented to the majority of viewers by the roving eye of multi-camera television. In fact, television has become the fulcrum of the business of modern sport. Over the last three to four decades, the athlete and televised sport have become inextricably linked in a cycle of booming success that has generated huge audiences and previously unimaginable amounts of money for sport. For the "golden eye" of television, read "golden goose." But it wasn't always so.

For most of the century, "live" meant being there, "immediacy" meant radio commentary, "news" meant the daily newspapers and the sports magazines. The best that could be offered by the moving image industry was weekly cinema newsreels and, at least for the Olympic Games, long-delayed official films. Of course, neither of these was available in the home. And it goes without saying there were no slo-mos, replays, or tracking cams; no close-ups, reverse angles, or pencil cams.

Pictures had to be painted for us through words—clearly articulated or beautifully written—reinforced by stunning moments of drama captured by the ubiquitous sports photographer.

The tide began to change in the fifties. It came in with frightening speed—and never went out again.

In 1948, grainy, obscure television images of the London Olympic Games were broadcast to a tiny audience of a few hundred pioneers in north London. Current technology did not permit the images to be recorded. The BBC paid the princely sum of 1,000 guineas for the privilege. The check was never cashed by the Games' organizing committee.

The technological torrent was in flood by 1956 for the Winter Games in Cortina. This was real television. But not everyone was convinced. Industry lore recounts that the torchbearer at the opening ceremony tripped over a television cable when entering the stadium. It took five minutes to relight the flame! Avery Brundage, the president of the International Olympic Committee, was not amused. In his classic comment on the unfortunate moment, Brundage insisted, "We've survived for sixty years without television; we can survive for another sixty."

In 1958, the Brooklyn Dodgers, New York's legendary baseball team, uprooted themselves and moved to the more lucrative environment of Los Angeles. Sports Illustrated said it marked the time when sport "lost its innocence forever." Nineteen fifty-eight was also the year when Johnny Unitas and the Baltimore Colts beat the New York Giants in a classic encounter on live television that went to eight minutes of overtime. The drama of the occasion, captured by television, transformed the public profile of American football.

By 1960, and the Olympic Games in Rome, television was able to transmit live events to a worldwide audience. So it was in 1962 for the soccer World Cup in Chile. The rest, as they say, is history.

The "golden goose" of television now produces astronomical income. For example, the worldwide rights fees for the summer Olympic Games have grown as follows:

	U.S. DOLLARS
Moscow 1980	101 million
Los Angeles 1984	287 million
Seoul 1988	403 million
Barcelona 1992	636 million
Atlanta 1996	900 + million
Sydney 2000	1100 + million

The all-powerful eye of television is illustrated by the statistics for media accreditation at major sporting events. The Atlanta Olympic Games' accreditations totaled 5,000 for the printed press and photographers, but more than 12,000 for the television broadcasters.

Television has understandably taken a dominant role in capturing the drama of sport. However, as evidenced by this fine publication and the breathtaking moments it displays, there will always be a place for the writer's finely crafted word and the photographer's stunning still image.

American sprinter Michael Johnson celebrates after shattering the world record in the 200-meter dash at the Atlanta Olympics. Johnson ran each 100-meter segment faster than the 100-meter world record set earlier in Atlanta by Canada's Donovan Bailey. (Mike Powell)

For better or worse, sport is now a modern-day spectacle of massive proportions. The athletes are the gladiators for an audience of billions, made ever more rapacious by all the wonders of the electronic age. And from what the digital gurus tell us, it certainly won't stop here.

The juggernaut is still rolling. Ring the bell if anyone wants to get off!

Stewart Binns, Trans World International

No sailboat? No matter, let the wind propel your kite. Here, a view of kitebuggying in action in Camber Sands, England. (Mike Hewitt)

Giancarlo Fisichella of Italy, who came in fourth at the Italian Formula One Grand Prix at the Monza circuit in Monza, Italy, in September 1997, flies through the air during qualifying. (Clive Mason)

• Before a Formula One Grand Prix, a photographer will spend three or more hours walking the circuit to investigate the most favorable positions.
• With cars racing between 150 and 200 mph, the photographer has only a fraction of a second to capture a car in the center of the frame and in focus. He must anticipate the moment by listening for the noise of the engines before the cars come into sight.

Making leaps and bounds: American Ralph Hill urges on his horse at the 1995 Advance Horse Trials in Atlanta. (Simon Bruty)

Revved up: Australian Darryl Beattie gets hurled from his Suzuki at the Spanish Motorcycle Grand Prix on May 12, 1996, at Jerez. (Michael Cooper)

Cyclist upended: Gil Cordoues of Cuba is discharged by his bicycle in the 4000-meter team race at the 1995 Pan Am Games, in Cuba. (Simon Bruty)

Man overboard! Charlie Swan encounters a difficult fence and is forced to make an involuntary dismount at the Cheltenham Racing Festival, in March 1996. (Dave Rogers)

Equipped with spikes on their hooves, horses race through the snow on a track in St. Moritz, Switzerland, in February 1997. (Mike Hewitt)

Ice storm: Biking over the ice on February 26, 1995, at the
Ice Speedway in Frankfurt, Germany. (Clive Brunskill)

THINKING BACK TO
WINNING GOLD

in the Super G at the 1998 Olympic Games in Nagano, Japan, I see myself in the finish area with my team feeling such elation and also shock. With so much injury in the last two years, even to make the U.S. team was an achievement, but to bring back a gold medal was incredibly wonderful—it has brought me so much pride and joy to win for my country.

It takes tunnel-vision focus to be the best, and sometimes I feel like I never want to race again—but most of the time I can't wait to get out there. When I race, I race to win. I relax, find a rhythm, and then charge through the course, like in Nagano. I attacked the course from top to bottom, pushing really hard and skiing very aggressively. Even when you are out with an injury, you have to think like that. You can't be afraid to risk; you must stay focused or else your brain wanders and loses direction. Fear can be the greatest obstacle, but you must replace the fear with the task at hand.

People have asked if I'll come back for the 2002 Olympics in Salt Lake City. I'm definitely taking next year off, but I don't think the opportunity to compete at such a high level on my home turf is one I want to miss. I've been set back by injuries, but I'm sure I'll have enough time to recover.

Like everything else in life, where there's a real up, there's also a real down. When you invest so much of yourself in your dream the toll is high and the continual damage causes mental as well as physical pain. Though the physio is tough, the daily progress keeps you going, and when the hard work pays off with an Olympic gold, it's a bright spot you carry around with you always. When you win, it affects your whole life—you bring it to your next race, your personal life, and those low moments so difficult to overcome. It gives you the confidence to smile and carry on.

Picabo Street

American downhill skier Picabo Street poses while training near home in Portland, Oregon, before winning an Olympic gold in Nagano, Japan. (Mike Powell)

Speed demon: Gerard Escoda, one of four Andorran athletes at the 1998 Winter Olympics at Nagano, Japan, hurtles downhill in the men's giant slalom. (Shaun Botterill)

P. 84–85: Czech skier Jaroslav Sakala soars in his final 90-kilometer jump at the 1998 Winter Olympics at Hakuba, Japan. (Al Bello)

Alexander Spitz of Germany falls and breaks his leg during the LW2 downhill alpine skiing race at the 1998 Paralympics in Nagano, Japan. (Alex Livesey)

• In downhill racing the photographer has an allotted position on the course from which he cannot move. This allows only milliseconds per competitor in which to take a photo—not to mention the fact that the skier may fall before reaching the photographer's viewpoint, destroying his opportunity altogether.

Blink and you'll miss it: American duo Christopher Thorpe and Gordy Sheer on their silver-medal two-man luge run at the 1998 Winter Olympics in Nagano, Japan. (Jamie Squire)

Four cyclists climb the precarious rim of the velodrome at the
4000-meter race at the 1995 Pan Am Games. (Simon Bruty)

A lone 250cc rider rounds the bend at dusk at the 1993 Spanish Motorcycle Grand Prix at Jarama. (Anton Want)

A rower glides through softly lit waters at the 1995
United States Rowing Championships. (Jamie Squire)

p. 92–93: Kenyan runner Daniel Komen, the world
record-holder at 3,000 meters, 2 miles, and
5,000 meters, silhouetted by the waning light of day
as he runs in his homeland in April 1997. (Simon Bruty)

p. 94–95: Choisty soars over Beechers Brook at the 1998
Martell Grand National at Aintree in England. (Ross Kinnaird)

British Formula One driver David Coulthard focuses on ensuring the resurgence of the McLaren-Mercedes team in February of the 1998 season. (Mark Thompson)

Trophy in hand, German racer Michael Schumacher and his Ferrari team celebrate their win in the Belgium Grand Prix in August of 1994. (Pascal Rondeau)

All is a blur as the France-1 team celebrates their bronze medal-winning performance at the 1998 Nagano Olympics. (Shaun Botterill)

Following bicycle tours is one of a sports photographer's greatest challenges.
- The Tour de France consists of twenty-one stages that are traversed over three weeks in the height of summer, during which cyclists have to pit their endurance against the plains of the Massif Centrale and the cool peaks of the Alps.
- It is very important for photographers to be mobile during the tour. Ideally, they should follow the cyclists throughout each day's race, a distance of sometimes more than 120 miles.
- Access to the cyclists' route is not restricted, but photographers have to make the most of their chances. A photographer can ride on the back of a motorbike ahead of the leaders, but this allows him only to shoot those at the head of the pack. There is not much variety in the type of shots from this position.
- The other positions lie along the route, where it is possible to capture all of the competitors as they pass and also shoot general views such as the following shot, taking in the beauty of the French landscape.

No time for second thoughts: Two cyclists cross railroad tracks before an oncoming train in the second leg of the 1996 Tour DuPont, on their way from Fredericksburg, Maryland, to Richmond, Virginia. (Al Bello)

p. 100–101: Awash in vibrant yellow, the eighth stage of the 1994 Tour de France, a 135-mile ride from Poitiers to Trelissac. Denmark's Bo Hamburger won the stage, but Spain's Miguel Indurain came through with his fourth consecutive Tour de France victory. (Pascal Rondeau)

Jeff Gordon qualifies for the 1997 UAW-GM Quality 500 Winston Cup race at Charlotte Motor Speedway, where he finished fifth, thereby collecting $4 million in prize money for the year. (David Taylor)

- For photographing auto racing, the shutter speed must be low enough to demonstrate the speed and movement of the car—the wheels should be blurred with the motion. If the shutter speed is too high, the photo will appear static.
- Panning along with the car as one opens the shutter also creates an image of motion by merging the background into hazy masses of color while keeping the car pin-sharp.

Going for gold: Runners tear up the track in the women's 10,000-meter heats at Olympic Stadium at the 1996 Olympics in Atlanta. (Nathan Bilow)

p. 104–105: Swedish Match in the 31,600-nautical-mile Whitbread Round-the-World race for the Volvo Trophy from Southampton back to Southampton. All nine boats finished this third leg from Fremantle to Sydney within an hour and twenty minutes of one another. (Stephen Munday)

p. 106–107: Mirage in motion: Ironman Triathalon competitors shimmer deceptively under the blistering heat of the Hawaii sun in the cycling portion of the 1995 race. (Mike Powell)

Cooling down the heat of anticipation, a swimmer splashes himself at the starting blocks of
the 200-meter breaststroke heats at the Atlanta Olympics. (Jed Jacobsohn)

On the run: a marathoner cools off during the 1995 Outdoor World I.A.A.F. Championships in Gothenburg, Sweden. (Michael Cooper)

Bubble boy: Belgium's Frederik Deburghgraeve on his way to the gold medal for the 100-meter breaststroke at the 1995 European Swimming Championships in Vienna, Austria. (Shaun Botterill)

American long-jumper Mike Powell screamed out in pain and then remained in the pit for two minutes after his sixth and final jump at the 1996 Olympic Games in Atlanta. (Gary M. Prior)

p. 112–113: Double exposure: A swimmer's goggles reflect in the water at the Puento Romano Hotel pool in Marbella, Spain. (Chris Cole)

p. 114–115: Ocean Rover crew man Jon Hirsch checks the mast above the assembled 1997 BT Global Challenge fleet moored in Cape Town at the end of stage four. Ocean Rover finished eighth in the competition. (Clive Mason)

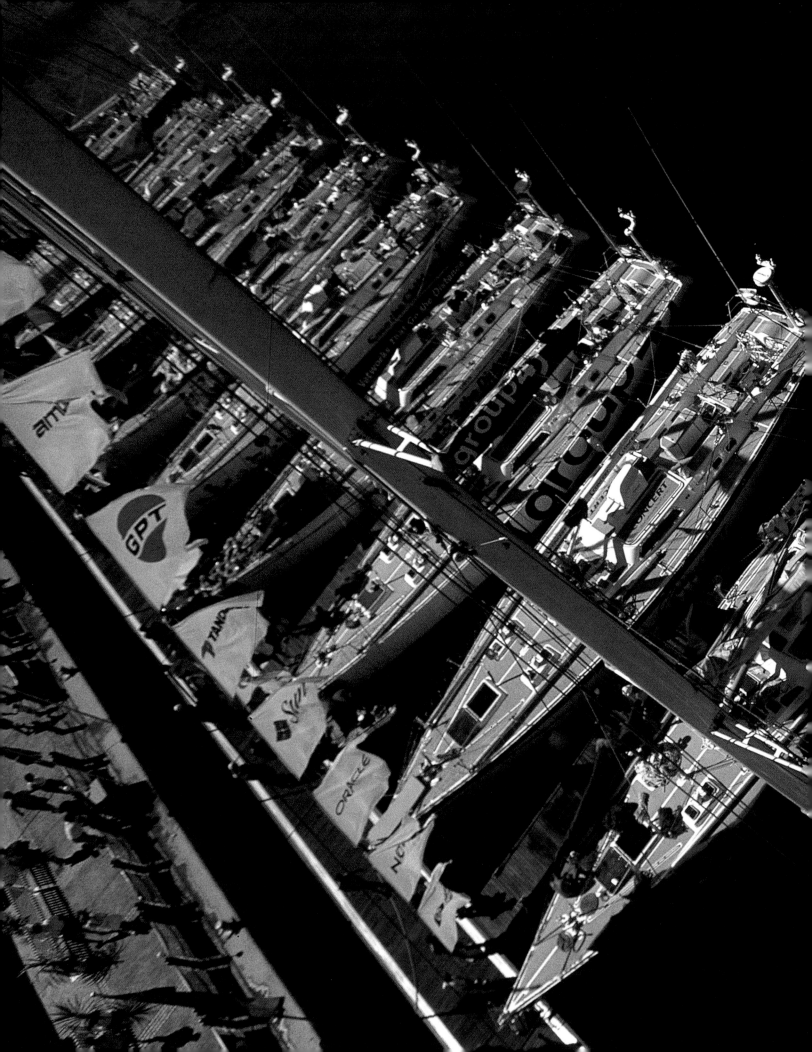

TEAM

SPIRIT

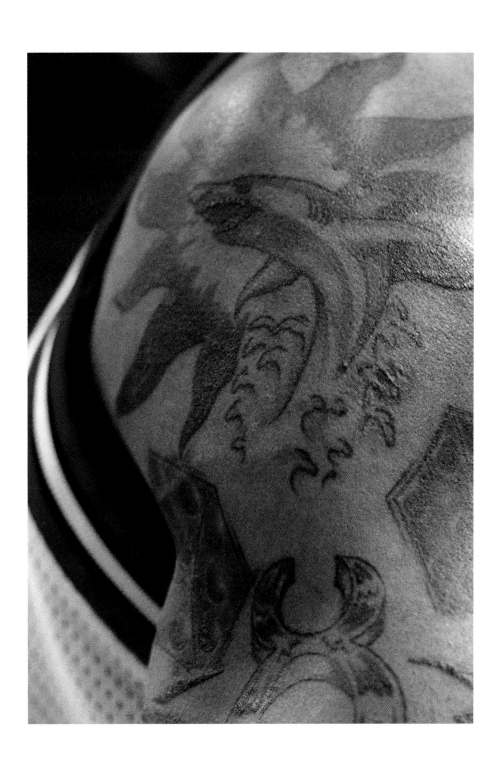

American Alexi Lalas grimaces and drops to the ground in pain after being fouled by Luis Roberto Alves in a 2–0 1997 U.S. Cup loss to Mexico at the Rose Bowl in Pasadena, California. (Elsa Hasch)

THE GREAT THING ABOUT SPORTS

is that it changes every day. No two events are the same, and once the match is over, you can never play it again. It's a moment in history with its own identity, its own spirit, and its own memories. Nothing else in the news business is quite like it. Covering wars may be exciting, but war correspondents will tell you that much of it entails sitting around waiting for the action to happen. And lately, government officials must hold your hand in controversial areas, a procedure bordering on censorship. Reporting on the White House or 10 Downing Street is a bit like watching a chess match. There are thrilling moments, but they are as rare as they are scintillating.

Sport, on the other hand, is always exciting, always different, always memorable. I will argue that if you watch enough baseball or soccer (two sports that are considered somewhat cerebral, or at least, lacking in constant, gut-wrenching action), you will see something every day that you had not seen before. It may be quirky, subtle, or comical, but watch enough of it and you become quite appreciative of the strategies. A colleague of mine once said that sports is the last bastion of photojournalism. You cannot set it up, you cannot manipulate it, and you cannot predict the result.

Sports photography has all the elements of the subject it covers: the thrill of the chase, the ultra-competitiveness of its participants, and the high-risk, high-reward stakes of creating the key picture. Add to that the sometimes messy conditions, the lack of access, and the silly rules that the governing bodies impose, and you have a battlefield on the sidelines equal to the skirmish you are covering. This is not an arena for the weak.

A noted American broadcaster said recently that while television records history in a continuous, banal way, still photography gives history its eternal high points. Last night's highlights show looks a lot like the night before; the still picture published in the morning paper or magazine lasts forever. Fans pore over such critical images recalling where they were, what they were feeling, and how it affected their lives. There is nothing like a great picture of an important play. (And remember—you cannot take the television to the washroom.)

Allsport has kept this lesson in mind for thirty years. Don't follow the pack; don't try to make the safe picture (leave that to the wire services); don't settle for the ordinary. Make the reader feel as if he were there. Give him a sense of place. Find the right light and wait for the picture to develop.

As a stock agency, Allsport is unparalleled. If you need an Olympic sprinter for a preview, Allsport has it. Looking for a star midfielder who just retired, Allsport has a dozen different images of him at play and at home. Need some obscure bowler in South Africa, Allsport has already discovered him.

As a wire service, Allsport has changed the way we cover sports. Can't afford to send a photographer to the Davis Cup in Romania, Allsport has two of them there. Need pickup from an auto race, Allsport has the crash and the winner's circle. Looking for a different angle on the tennis court, Allsport put a camera in the net.

For Allsport, it's always been more than just coverage. It's about creating spectacular images, capturing key moments in sport that will be remembered for all time.

Steve Fine,
Picture Editor, Sports Illustrated

UCLA fans in Pauley Pavilion celebrate a 74–67 victory over Oregon to give UCLA the 1997 Pac-10 college basketball title. (Elsa Hasch)

The Washington Wizards opened the $200 million MCI Center, with President Clinton in attendance, with a 95–78 victory over the Seattle SuperSonics on December 2, 1997. (Jamie Squire)

Kobe Bryant of the Los Angeles Lakers shows Minnesota Timberwolves defenders his gravity-defying powers at Great Western Forum in Inglewood, California, on November 19, 1997. (Jed Jacobsohn)

Ian Wright of Arsenal leaping high for a kick in a 3–1 loss to Blackburn on December 14, 1997 in north London. (Corey Ross)

• Soccer photographers have limited access to positions on the pitch and must stay where they are allocated. From that one spot, a photographer must be able to follow fast-paced, erratic play, catching goals, celebrations, fouls, and free-kicks—not to mention dealing with TV cameras blocking the way.

A basketball player goes for a reverse slam in front of the Pacific Ocean on the California coast. (Mike Powell)

England left-arm spin bowler Phil Tufnell celebrates his seven-wicket haul in the first inning of the sixth test against Australia on August 22, 1997. (Clive Mason)

It's all in the eyes: Great Britain's Colin Jackson with Union Jack contact lenses at the 1997 World Championships in Athens, Greece. Jackson took home a silver in the 110-meter hurdles. (Clive Brunskill)

The San Francisco 49ers huddle up in an 11–7 loss to the New Orleans Saints at home in 3Com Park during a game in which future Hall of Fame wide receiver Jerry Rice became the NFL's leader in career receiving yardage. (Al Bello)

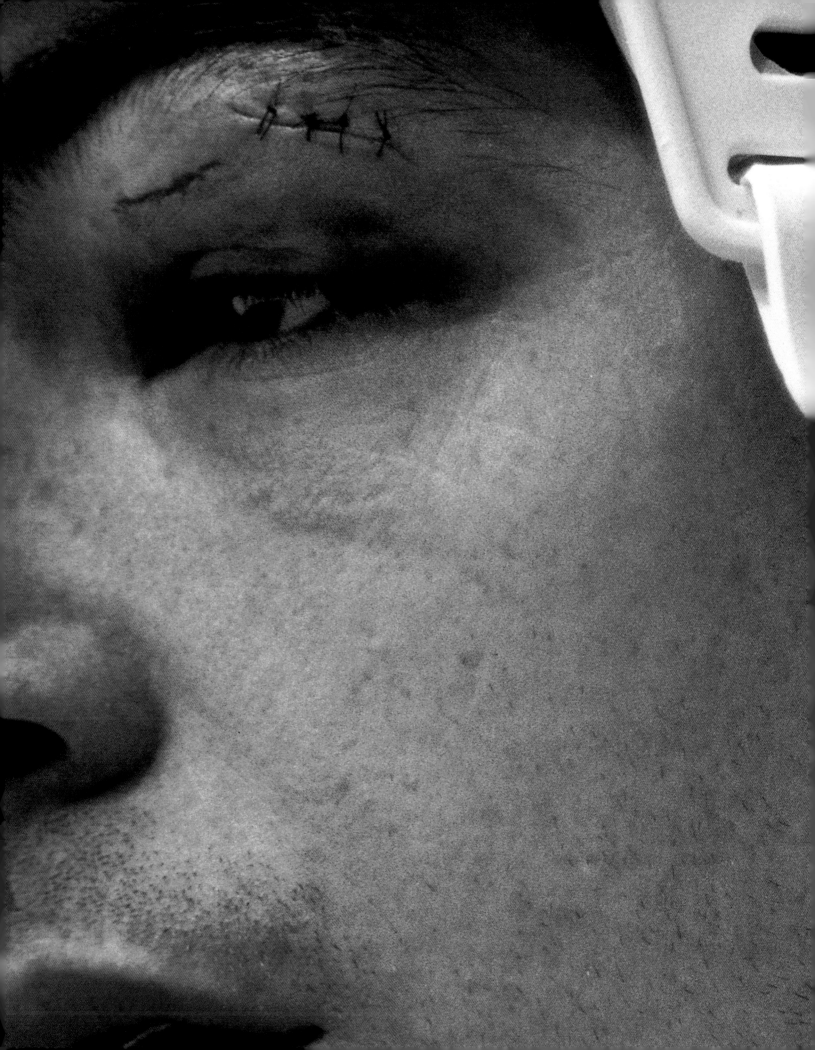

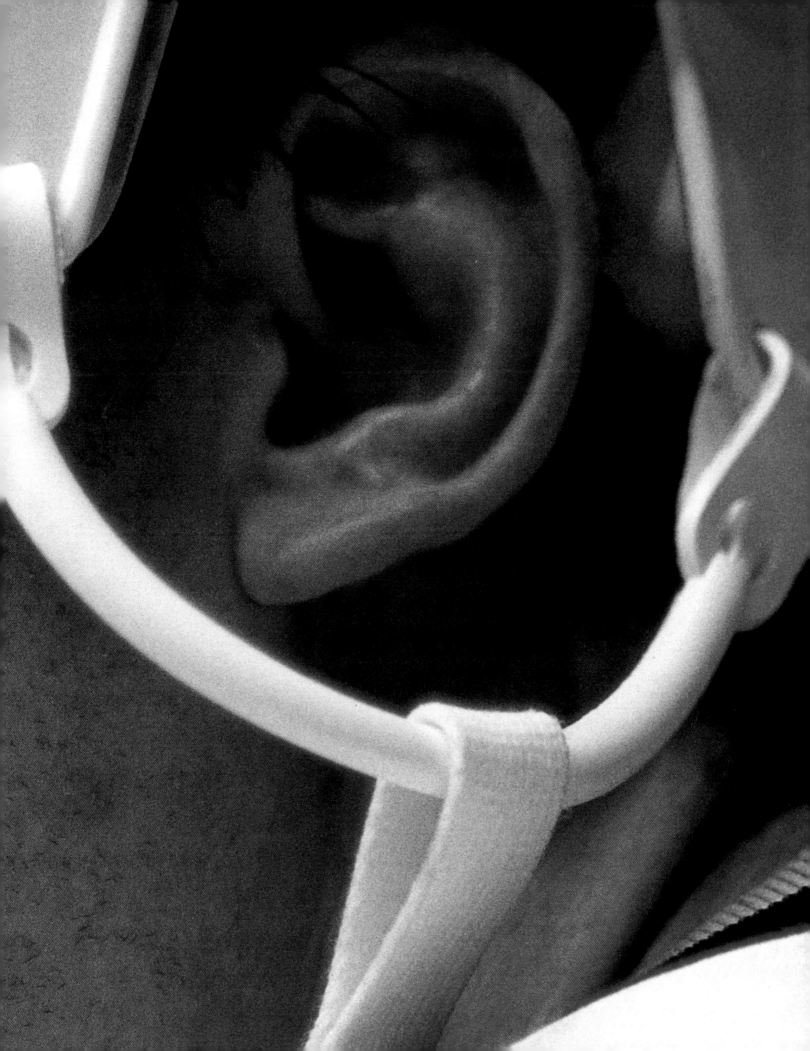

Two players give it their all in the United States' 3–2 comeback win against silver medallists South Korea in women's field hockey at the Atlanta Olympics. (Stu Forster)

p. 128–129: The bloodied and swollen eye of Los Angeles Kings defenseman Sean O'Donnell, suffered in a 5–2 home win over the Tampa Bay Lightning on November 6, 1997. (Aubrey Washington)

Japanese goalie Dusty Imoo saves a shot from Austrian Richard Nasheim on the way to a 3–3 (3–2) shootout win at the Nagano Olympics, giving Japan their first Olympic ice hockey victory since 1976. (Brian Bahr)

New Jersey Devils goalie Martin Brodeur holds Montreal to a single goal in a 4–1 win on February 15, 1997. (Robert Laberge)

p. 134–135: The USA's Todd Hosmer steals the ball from fast-approaching Sergi Pederoi of Spain at the World Water Polo Championship held at the Challenge Stadium in Perth, Australia, in January 1998. Despite Hosmer's efforts, Spain beat the USA 5–4. (Al Bello)

p. 136–137: Heads up: The synchronized swimming team of Spain displays its watery grace at the World Swimming Championships at Challenge Stadium in Perth, Australia, January 10, 1998. (Todd Warshaw)

SINCE I WAS A SMALL BOY

growing up just outside of Montreal, Quebec, I have been surrounded by sports photography. My dad, Denis, was the team photographer for both the Montreal Expos and the Montreal Canadiens so there were always sports photographs everywhere I looked.

A photograph can tell a thousand words, but sometimes one word can describe the feeling of a great picture, or even the feelings of the athlete himself. I've looked at thousands of photographs in my life, but the one thing I always focus on is the eyes, the window to the soul. Through the expression on an athlete's face, you can almost read what's running through his mind, whether he's nervous, frightened, or excited, whether he wishes he were somewhere else, or screaming, "bring it on!" You can learn a lot in the split second the lens is open.

As a kid I had three posters on my bedroom walls: Sean Burke, Ron Hextall, and Patrick Roy. It seemed so odd to go out and play against them when I first broke into the NHL. These days I don't think about it anymore, but the first couple of times I kept thinking, "Wow, these are the guys I have on my wall." It's just fun now, to go out and compete against such great goaltenders—and even more fun to beat them.

Obviously, my dad has taken a large number of pictures of me while playing for the New Jersey Devils. These are always fun to look at. Just as if I were looking at a picture of another athlete, I study the facial expression. I've seen so many great pictures of great goaltenders, I can't help but compare them to pictures of myself. Do I look like Bernie Parent, Terry Sawchuk, Gump Worsley, Ken Dryden, or Glenn Hall? It's always amusing to compare pictures of the great goaltenders to mine, but I also use them as a learning tool. I visualize their positioning and try to imitate them when I play. Looking at photos of myself and comparing them to these memorable images helps me learn and ultimately improve my game.

A photographer constantly attempts to capture the best possible images, and the greatest feeling is being acknowledged for this achievement. It is always nice to look at a great photo and see my dad's name next to it. My all-time favorite picture is one my dad took the year I was born, showing the goal scored by Paul Henderson during the 1972 Summit Series versus the Russians. It is an unbelievable photo; you see the Canadiens celebrating and the Russians crying, completely overwhelmed by emotion. Twenty-five years ago that picture was publicized all over the world, and people still talk about it today. It is probably his greatest work, and it makes me enormously proud.

Martin Brodeur with Kevin Dessart

Unfazed by a passing cruise ship as they battle it out in picturesque St. Kitts, the Australian cricket team takes on the West Indies President's XI team in April 1995. (Clive Mason)

• A cricket side has eleven players with two umpires governing the play. The players are situated across a field of approximately 80–100 meters. From his position, the photographer must be ready to take in all of the players at any given time, at any spot within this entire area.

• A cricket match may last anywhere between one and five days. A photographer may find he is running out of time to get the pictures he needs, and he may have long periods of waiting between spurts of action. Much patience is required.

Quarterback John Friesz of the Seattle Seahawks drops back to pass in the golden Denver sky in a 31–27 comeback victory over the Broncos at Mile High Stadium on December 12, 1995. (Al Bello)

Paul Medley of rugby's 1997 Super League champions Bradford Bulls is wrestled to a halt by Denis Betts. (Graham Chadwick)

• Photographers at rugby games are given more freedom to "run the line," making them able to adjust their positions according to the intermittent nature of the play. While scrums slow the action down, the photographer must place himself in a position that depicts the break in play telling the story of the match.

Air Force quarterback Beau Morgan has his face mask grabbed by Karl Ballard of Colorado State in a 27–20 home loss for Air Force in 1995. (Mike Powell)

New York Yankees closer John Wetteland gets mobbed by his teammates after recording the final out of the 1996 World Series with a 3–2 win over the Atlanta Braves at Yankee Stadium. (Doug Pensinger)

Antonio Freeman of the Green Bay Packers celebrates a touchdown by leaping into the arms of fellow wide receiver Robert Brooks, though the Packers lost Super Bowl XXXII to the Denver Broncos 31–24 at Qualcomm Stadium in San Diego, California. (Al Bello)

The United States women's ice hockey team pose for a victory shot following their gold medal-winning performance at the Nagano Olympics. (Al Bello)